Eggs in the Hay

Clive Percival
Illustrated by Andrew Plant

How many eggs are in the hay?
How many eggs will hatch today?

3

The first egg cracks.
Mother duck quacks.

Look! One little duckling!

The second egg cracks.
Mother duck quacks.

Look! Two little ducklings!

The third egg cracks.
Mother duck quacks.

8

Look! Three little ducklings!

The fourth egg cracks.
Mother duck quacks.

Look! Four little ducklings!

How many eggs were in the hay?
How many ducklings hatched today?